EDGE
BOOKS

BMX EXTREME

BMX
DESIGN AND EQUIPMENT

by Brian D. Fiske

Consultant:
Keith Mulligan
Editor/Photographer
TransWorld BMX Magazine

Capstone
press

Mankato, Minnesota

Edge Books are published by Capstone Press
151 Good Counsel Drive, P.O. Box 669, Mankato, Minnesota 56002
www.capstonepress.com

Library of Congress Cataloging-in-Publication Data
Fiske, Brian D.
　　BMX design and equipment / by Brian D. Fiske.
　　p. cm.—(Edge books. BMX extreme)
　　Summary: Describes the bicycles and equipment used in the sport of bicycle
motocross.
　　Includes bibliographical references and index.
　　ISBN 0-7368-2432-4 (hardcover)
　　1. BMX bikes—Design and construction—Juvenile literature. 2. BMX bikes—
Equipment and supplies—Juvenile literature. 3. Bicycle motocross. [1. BMX bikes.
2. Bicycle motocross.] I. Title. II. Series.
TL437.5.B58F57 2004
629.227'2—dc22　　　　　　　　　　　　　　　　　2003013709

Editorial Credits

Angela Kaelberer, editor; Enoch Peterson, series designer; Jason Knudson,
　　book designer; Jo Miller, photo researcher

Photo Credits

Capstone Press/Gary Sundermeyer, 22–23
Corbis/Vince Streano, 12
Getty Images/Adam Pretty, 18; Elsa, 5, 21; Mark Mainz, 17
Keith Mulligan/Transworld BMX, cover, 7, 10, 15, 16, 20, 26, 27
Scot "OM" Breithaupt, 9
SportsChrome-USA/Rob Tringali Jr., 25, 29

1 2 3 4 5 6 09 08 07 06 05 04

Table of Contents

Chapter 1:
Bicycle Motocross 4

Chapter 2:
Early BMX Bikes 8

Chapter 3:
Today's Bikes 14

Chapter 4:
Equipment 24

Diagram: Freestyle Bike 22

Glossary 30

Read More 31

Useful Addresses 31

Internet Sites 32

Index 32

Bicycle Motocross

On August 18, 2002, BMX fans filled the stands of the First Union Complex in Philadelphia, Pennsylvania. The fans waited to see which riders would win medals in the park event at the X Games.

Ryan Nyquist had some bad luck in the middle of his first run. One of the crank arms on his bike broke. Nyquist could not pedal the bike with the broken crank arm.

Nyquist did not panic. He borrowed Allan Cooke's bike for his second run. Some of the people watching thought the unfamiliar bike might cause Nyquist to have a bad run.

Learn about:

- Ryan Nyquist
- Design changes
- Upgraded parts

Ryan Nyquist rode a borrowed bike at the 2002 X Games.

Nyquist proved them wrong. He did a double truckdriver, a rocket no-hander, and finished with a 720 over the spine. The judges rewarded his performance with a gold medal.

What happened to Nyquist that day shows how important equipment is to a BMX rider. Even the best rider cannot do tricks or win races without a sturdy, dependable bike.

BMX Equipment

BMX equipment has changed since the sport began. BMX began with simple, homemade equipment. As the sport became more popular, companies worked to make quality, high-tech equipment.

Today, BMX riders have many more choices in equipment than early riders did. Bikes made of strong, lightweight materials give racers an added advantage. Riders can choose upgraded parts that improve the bikes' handling and speed. Clothes, gloves, and helmets are all designed to fit the needs of BMX riders.

Today, clothes and helmets are designed for BMX riders.

CHAPTER 2

Early BMX Bikes

BMX was started in the early 1970s by riders who were too young to race motorcycles. These riders raced bicycles on motocross tracks.

Schwinn Stingray

Most of the first BMX riders used Schwinn Stingrays. Several features made the Stingray good for BMX riding. Like today's BMX bikes, the Stingray had 20-inch (51-centimeter) wheels. The bike's steel frame was strong enough to handle the bumps and jumps of the dirt motocross tracks. The Stingray's tall handlebars were tilted slightly back. This position gave riders more control on the tracks.

Learn about:

- Schwinn Stingray
- First BMX bikes
- Early gear

Tilted handlebars gave BMX riders more control on dirt tracks.

The Stingray was not perfect for BMX. The bike had a large banana-shaped seat. BMX riders usually do not sit on the seat during races. Instead, they stand on the pedals. The Stingray's large seat added unneeded weight to the bike. The Stingray's tires were too smooth to grip the rough tracks. Riders often crashed.

Red Line Engineering made one of the first BMX frames.

The biggest problem with the Stingray was its front fork. This part holds the front wheel. The fork also works with the handlebars to turn the front wheel. The Stingray's narrow front fork was not strong. It often bent during crashes or big jumps.

Rider Changes

As BMX became more popular, riders changed their bikes to make them better for racing. They took off the fenders and chain guards. They added bigger, stronger forks and knobby tires that gripped both dirt and mud. There were no BMX companies, so riders made their own parts. Some riders sold these parts to other riders.

In 1974, a motorcycle frame company called Red Line Engineering made the first manufactured BMX part. The part was a strong fork made of a material called chromoly steel alloy. Red Line quickly sold 200,000 forks. The company soon left the motorcycle business and became a BMX company.

Some early BMX riders wore motorcycle helmets.

FACT:

Red Line Engineering is now called Redline Bicycles. The company still makes BMX bikes and sponsors its own racing team.

In May 1974, a company called Webco made the first production bike frame designed for BMX riding. Yamaha, Kawasaki, and other companies soon made their own BMX bikes. The days of racing Schwinn Stingrays were over.

Clothes and Gear

Crashes are a part of BMX racing. Riders need clothing and equipment that protect them during crashes. The clothing also should allow riders to easily move and pedal.

Like the first bikes, the clothes worn by early BMX racers were not designed for BMX riding. The riders used whatever they could find. Early riders wore heavy boots, jeans, and gloves. They protected their heads with motorcycle helmets. Some riders even wore gardening gloves to protect their hands.

CHAPTER 3

Today's Bikes

All BMX bikes have the same basic parts, but there are differences. Some bikes have features that make them better for racing or freestyle. Riders also can add parts and equipment to improve the bikes' comfort or style.

Frames

The frame is one of the most important parts of a BMX bike. All other parts connect to the frame.

At least nine metal tubes form the frame. These parts include the top tube, the down tube, the seat tube, and the head tube. Other tubes are the bottom bracket, two chainstays, and two seatstays. Some frames have more tubes for extra support.

Learn about:

- Basic parts
- Racing equipment
- Freestyle parts

All parts connect to
the bike's frame.

Most racing bikes are made of aluminum.

Many racing bikes are made of a strong, lightweight metal called aluminum. Lightweight bikes allow riders to reach higher speeds. Lightweight bikes are also easier to handle.

Freestyle bikes need sturdier frames than racing bikes do. Most freestyle bikes are made of chromoly steel alloy. This strong material helps keep the frame from breaking during jumps and tricks.

Pedals

BMX riders use one of two types of pedals. Some racers use clipless pedals. These pedals have a metal or plastic part called a cleat that attaches to the bottom of the shoe. The cleat holds the foot on the pedal and allows the rider to pedal faster.

Most freestyle riders and some racers use platform pedals, which are also called flat pedals. These pedals are flat and wide. Each pedal may have many small pins on its surface. The pins can be moved up or down to help the rider's foot grip the pedal.

Most freestyle bikes have platform pedals.

17

Freestyle bikes have tires that grip smooth surfaces.

Wheels, Tires, and Brakes

BMX wheels are smaller than those on other types of bikes. Most BMX bikes have 20-inch (51-centimeter) wheels.

Riders use different types of tires depending on the type of riding they do. Knobby tires have many bumps and grooves that help racing bikes grip the dirt. Freestyle riders use wider, smoother tires. The freestyle tires grip ramps, parking lots, and other smooth surfaces.

A cable runs from the brake lever to the brakes. Squeezing the lever pulls the cable, which closes the brakes down on the rim of the wheel. Most racing bikes have brakes only on the rear wheel. Some freestyle bikes have brakes on both the front and rear wheels. Freestyle riders use the front brakes to do tricks.

Other Parts

Riders add other equipment suited for the type of riding they do. A racing bike has padding on the top tube, the top of the handlebar, and the stem. The stem connects the handlebar to the fork. A racing bike also needs a plate on the front to show the racer's number.

A racing bike has the racer's number on the front.

Many freestyle bikes have pegs attached to the wheels.

Freestyle bikes do not need pads or a numberplate, but they have other equipment. Many freestyle bikes have pegs attached to the front and rear wheels. Riders use the pegs to do peg stalls, peg grinds, and other tricks. Freestyle bikes also have a detangler. This part allows the handlebars to spin all the way around without tangling the brake cables.

Freestyle Bike

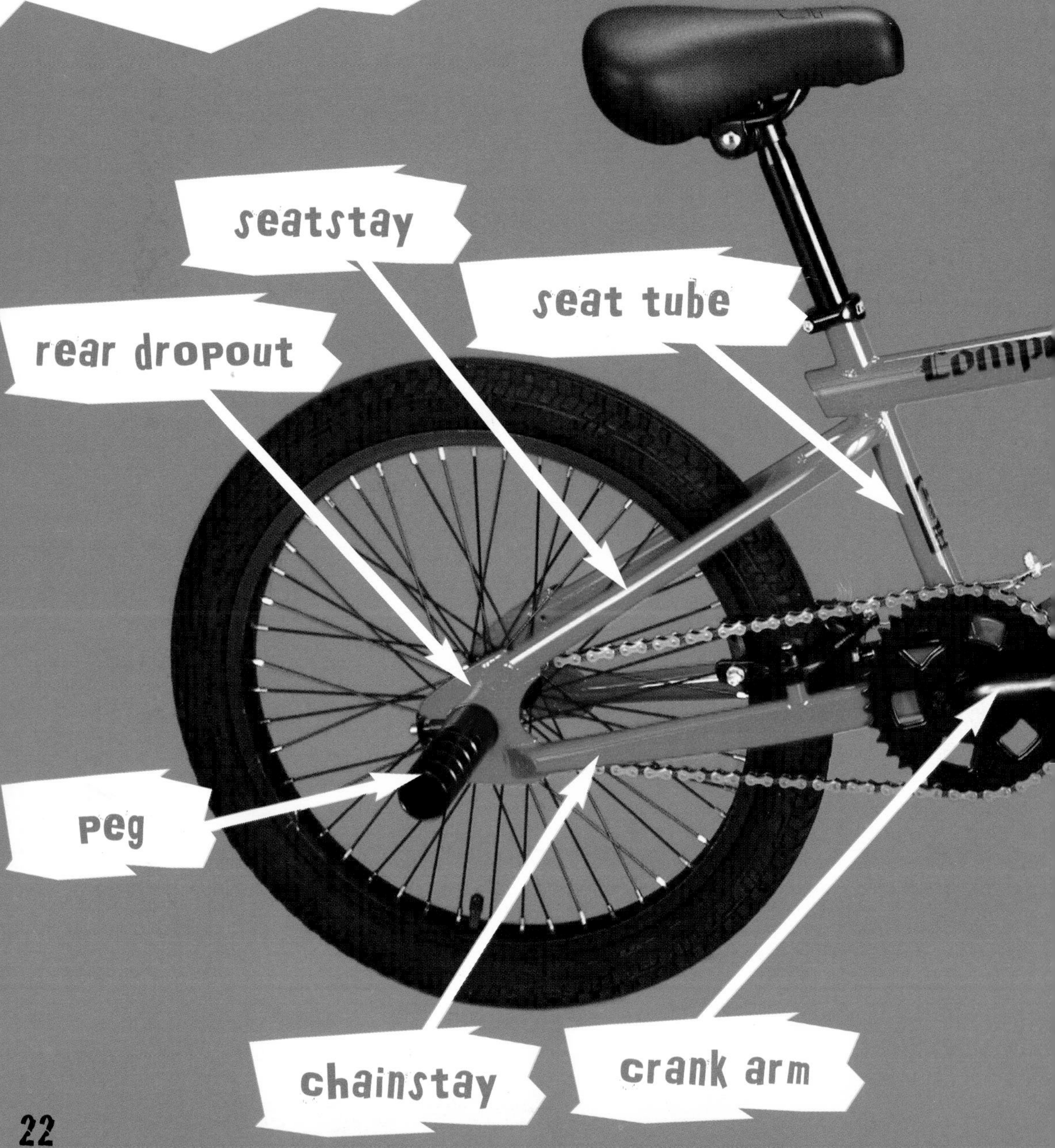

seatstay

seat tube

rear dropout

Compe

peg

chainstay

crank arm

brake cable

brake lever

top tube

detangler

head tube

fork

down tube

platform pedals

23

CHAPTER 4

Equipment

Next to the bike, clothing and protective gear are most important to a rider. Both racers and freestyle riders need clothing and equipment that keep them comfortable and safe.

A helmet is a rider's most important piece of protective gear. Most racers wear full-face helmets. These motorcycle-style helmets help protect a racer's head and face during crashes. Some freestyle riders also wear full-face helmets. Other freestyle riders wear helmets that cover only the top and back of the head.

Learn about:

- Helmets
- Clothes
- Shoes

Some freestyle riders wear helmets that cover only part of the head.

The only riders who do not always need helmets are flatland riders. These freestyle riders do tricks on parking lots and other flat, paved surfaces. They do not do jumps, so they are less likely to be hurt.

Clothing

BMX organizations set rules about the clothing racers wear. All racers must wear long pants and long-sleeved shirts. Racers' clothes are often made of lightweight materials that dry quickly and keep the skin cool. The pants may have built-in pads on the shins, knees, and hips to protect riders who fall.

Flatland freestyle riders do not always wear helmets.

Freestyle riders often wear gloves to protect their hands.

Freestyle riders have more freedom to wear what they want. Many freestyle riders wear short-sleeved shirts with either shorts or long pants. Their clothing should fit comfortably but not too loosely. Loose clothing may become caught in the bike's chain or on the seat or handlebars.

Other Equipment

Other protective gear includes gloves and pads. Many riders wear gloves to protect their hands and fingers. Both racers and freestyle riders often wear pads on their knees, shins, and elbows to protect them if they crash.

Both racers and freestyle riders should wear shoes that completely cover their feet. Most riders wear shoes with rubber soles that grip the pedals, giving the rider better control. Some racers wear shoes with hard, stiff soles. These soles support racers' feet as they pedal.

BMX equipment has come a long way from the equipment invented and produced by early riders. Today, riders can easily find equipment that lets them ride well, look good, and stay safe.

Elbow, knee, and shin pads protect riders who crash.

Glossary

aluminum (uh-LOO-mi-nuhm)—a strong, lightweight metal used to make racing bike frames

chromoly (kroh-MAWL-ee)—a mixture of metals used to make freestyle bike frames

detangler (dee-TANG-luhr)—a part on the front of the bike that allows the handlebars to spin without tangling the brake cables

frame (FRAYM)—the body of a bike

freestyle (FREE-stile)—a type of BMX riding that focuses on tricks, stunts, and jumps

motocross (MOH-toh-kross)—a sport in which people race motorcycles on dirt tracks

Read More

Deady, Kathleen W. *BMX Bikes.* Wild Rides! Mankato, Minn.: Capstone Press, 2002.

Dick, Scott. *BMX.* Radical Sports. Chicago: Heinemann Library, 2003.

Vieregger, K. E. *BMX Biking.* X-treme Sports. Edina, Minn.: Abdo, 2003.

Useful Addresses

American Bicycle Association
P.O. Box 718
Chandler, AZ 85244

National Bicycle League
3958 Brown Park Drive, Suite D
Hilliard, OH 43026

TransWorld BMX
1421 Edinger Avenue, Suite D
Tustin, CA 92780

Internet Sites

FactHound offers a safe, fun way to find Internet sites related to this book. All of the sites on FactHound have been researched by our staff.

Here's how:

1. Visit *www.facthound.com*
2. Type in this special code **0736824324** for age-appropriate sites. Or enter a search word related to this book for a more general search.
3. Click on the **Fetch It** button.

FactHound will fetch the best sites for you!

Index

brakes, 19, 21

clothing, 6, 13, 24, 26–27

fork, 11, 20
frame, 8, 11, 13, 14, 16
freestyle bikes, 14, 16, 19, 21

handlebars, 8, 11, 20, 21, 27
helmet, 6, 13, 24, 26

manufacturers, 6, 11, 13

padding, 20, 21, 26, 28
pedals, 10, 17, 28

racing bikes, 11, 13, 14, 16, 19, 20

safety, 13, 24, 26, 27, 28
Schwinn Stingray, 8, 10–11, 13

tires, 10, 11, 19
tracks, 8, 10

wheels, 8, 11, 19, 21

X Games, 4, 6